SEVEN BRIDGES

To Bonnie

Turning
Adversity Into Victory

Best of all Bridges

Dessa Reed

Dessa Byrd Reed

SEVEN BRIDGES
TURNING ADVERSITY INTO VICTORY

Copyright © 2003 by Dessa Byrd Reed

Deer Publishing
Post Office Box 3144
Palm Desert, Ca. 92261

Cover design by Robert Howard

Printed 05 04 03 ♥ 10 9 8 7 6 5 4 3 2 1

Publisher's Cataloging-in-Publication
(Provided by Quality Books, Inc.)

Reed, Dessa Byrd
    Seven bridges : turning adversity into victory /
Dessa Byrd Reed. -- 1st ed.
    p. cm.
    LCCN 2003091458
    ISBN 0-9678767-4-5

    1. Conduct of life--Poetry. 2. Success--Poetry.
I. Title.

PS3618.E434S48 2003   811'.6
                             QB133-1305

ACKNOWLEDGMENTS

I am grateful for all the "teachers" I have had since I first started writing poetry. These educators include my instructors at seminars, speakers at conferences, facilitators at critique groups, poets at workshops, as well as the people and things that appear every day to teach me life's lessons.

I have learned from some of the best poets in the world by reading their work or by hearing them perform in person. I have learned from those who have critiqued my poetry (even when I *knew* they were wrong!) As you will see from some of the poems in this book, I have also learned from a worm, flag, blood, shopping carts, a Monet painting, and from dozens of individuals and situations that have either blessed me or challenged me. I am especially grateful for the friends who loved and supported me as I moved over each new bridge. That turned a learning experience into firm but gentle growth—the best kind there is.

May it always be thus....

To my daughter
Kathy
Who walks my
SEVEN BRIDGES
With me

CONTENTS

BRIDGES TO TRAVEL

SPIRITUAL BRIDGES

SILLY BRIDGES I HAVE CROSSED

PERSONAL BRIDGES

I love the symbolism of a bridge. It is a metaphor for life—a moment-by-moment crossing over from one thought to another. Just about everything we do and every relationship we have are connections of some kind—bridges to people and places—past or future. Like a covered bridge, some of our personal bridges need tender protection. Others are open and expansive in order to sail across with the traffic. Even a rickety bridge can be crossed safely when conveyed with an attitude of healing and hope.

Poetry has taught me to see in symbols. When I first started journaling some of my deepest insights during many months of recovery from a near-fatal automobile accident, I noticed a colorful butterfly with its gentle, graceful touch. The word *touch* became a synonym for just about everything in my life. An early poem, THE BUTTERFLY TOUCH, inspired the title of my first book. I noticed that most of the poems I wrote seemed to fit into seven categories of *touches*.

In putting together this second book of poems, essays, and narrative, my new poems settled into those same categories. Only this time I envisioned *bridges* everywhere, symbolizing how expansive my life has become since my first feeble attempts at poetry. I have learned not to be afraid to cross a new bridge that might seem shrouded in the unknown. Often the other side has unimagined adventure and the journey can be exhilarating. I found these latest poems collected themselves into SEVEN BRIDGES.

This is really a self-help book—much more than a collection of my latest poems. Because I have come so far in my poetic rebirth, I hope to share some of my insights into how I was able to turn tragedy into treasure—adversity into victory.

Many people are looking for what I have discovered, synchronization with my destination or, put into spiritual terms, oneness with God. Sounds corny perhaps, but it is an idea that is about as powerful as we can experience.

As you read SEVEN BRIDGES I hope you feel its focus:

- Inspiration from a writer who has actually crossed over a life-threatening bridge and made it safely to the other side with a new awareness of an unknown ability.

- Encouragement that within each one of us is a poet ready to be released from hiding under the bridge of repression.

- Poems that dance on the bridge.

Dessa Byrd Reed

RUBY BRIDGES

I think I fell in love with the word, *bridge* when I heard the story of Ruby Bridges. During Black History Month I watched a television program about Ruby who was the first black child to be enrolled in an all-white school under court order in 1962. The movie showed how six-year-old Ruby prayed her way through the hate-filled crowds as she entered school. Also, about the same time, a televised biography of Norman Rockwell, our much loved American artist and magazine illustrator, included the now famous painting of a little black girl walking to school with United States Marshals protecting her. Mr. Rockwell had perfectly captured the scene that was both tender and terrifying. That graphic picture appeared on a LOOK magazine cover January 14, 1964.

I was touched by the amazing courage of Ruby Bridges and her family as they prayerfully prepared each day to meet the challenge of integration. It is emotional experiences like this one that bring forth poetry from me. The following poem almost wrote itself after watching those two powerful programs.

Ruby Bridges literally became a bridge to integration in this country—a bridge to personal growth for Ruby and her family, and a bridge to poetic appreciation for me personally. That is why the title and focus of this book came from a new love and respect for the idea of how all-encompassing and far reaching a connection or transition called a bridge can be.

Perhaps you will find a blessing bridge as well.

3

RUBY BRIDGES

Black beauty of bravery
U.S. Marshals fore
U.S. Marshals aft
A Ship of State
Floating freedom
Beyond color
Into the tides of progress
Anchored in equality

Our six-year-old sacrifice
Carries no cross
No crown of thorns encircles
Her white-ribboned pigtails
No blood stains her
Store-bought dress
Yet she walks through the same
Hate hissing cat calls
And arched backs
Of mob mentality
Whose fear of change
And dying traditions
Turn blue-blooded white faces red
Without Stars and Stripes

Marching as a soldier of society
A dark dot in history
Too innocent to be afraid

MOMENTS

ON THE

BRIDGE

LIVE IN THE MOMENT! I had been hearing (and saying) that for years but I actually learned the importance of living on the bridge of NOW from a wheelchair. I couldn't jump up and go shopping, so instead, I wrote and I wrote. To my amazement my writing turned into poetry. Now fully recovered, I still try to remember to stay in the moment—and to write. My hope is that you too will find inspiration and healing in the power of the pencil (or computer).

A poem or a story cocoons in everything we see every moment. Poetry is writing about life. The subjects are endless—standing in line at the bank, sitting in a small musty library or funky cafe, walking across a 115 degree parking lot, watching a sun rise—all simple everyday events made poetic by personal observation and our own unique word combinations. The subject can be as sad as a world tragedy (9/11/01) or as happy as seeing a new baby. You will find a poem about every single one of these experiences throughout my SEVEN BRIDGES. What we write about, good or bad, is from our special view on the bridge.

One day, when walking near the beach, I noticed luxurious homes on one side of me and on the other elegant boats moored to elaborate docks. I could have written about the homes, the boats, the scenery, but what brought forth a poem that day was that almost everyone I met was talking on a cell phone oblivious to all the beauty around them. Bridging that moment with humor released the next poem, *Addiction*. I wrote it in the first person since I have been guilty of the same sin so I couldn't sound preachy about other's obvious self-absorption. That is a poetry fundamental—to make a powerful point without sounding sanctimonious.

7

ADDICTION

Stronger than cigarettes
Numbing like alcohol
Promises the world
Makes me feel twice as tall
Addicted to this thing
Life will never be the same

Walks down the street
Talks inside my car
Rings in a restaurant
Regardless where we are
Addicted to this thing
Life will never be the same

Breaking my habit
I'll try any cure
Hit menu for mute
Turn it off for sure
Addicted to this thing
Life will never be the same

I walk 12 steps out the door
First day sober of phone
Takes cold turkey courage
To leave my mobile at home
Free at last from this thing
Life will never be the same

PAPER TRAILS

The cozy county library, whose
battered books line
sagging shelves, is my
door to dreams
unlived.

The smell of aging pages
settles on my clothes like
smoke from a dying fire.
Smoldering desire to absorb
every word of every book
on every shelf
flame-leaps into restless wandering
down dusty trails in this
library forest.

Paper words
recycle into my soul
accepting ageless wisdom,
rejecting outmoded ideas.

Each found book
a new best friend
opening its review to mine.

MIDWIFE TO THE DAWN

The sun unleashes
Infant colors
As pink cheeks of a baby dawn
Peek
Over the cradle of mountains

Sunrise sings
A lullaby to the desert sky
Moldy clouds
Threaten rain
Like false labor

The birth of my day
Painless
Effortless
Expectant
Promises progress

Delivers fulfillment

SUMMER MELT-DOWN

I walk across the parking lot
in 115 degree heat
asphalt 153 under my feet
its black goo sticks
like chewing gum on a tread mill
Locals in air-conditioned autos
obey the law of our desert jungle
stop for every walking
hot heap of fevered flesh

My car breathes its torrid breath
onto exposed extremities
as I poke a toe into
the Chrysler crematory
Legs and leather seats
meld into a crazy glue marriage
Fingers dance on the steering wheel
until a squall of cool air
finally conquers August

at least for the moment

Sitting by the pool one searing day, I looked up to witness a fierce date palm patiently waiting to attack (or so it appeared). Our imagination can look at almost any object and explode with adventure and animation. Even during the most challenging times, I have found that writing poetry is a healthy habit. Especially so in the middle of the night when life's bridges seem to be the darkest, creating a poem can figuratively and literally bring the light.

I have often picked up paper and pencil kept by my bedside and written in the darkness, only to find that the next morning my scribbles were either brilliant (sort of) or brainless. Either way, the effort usually brings moments of peace.

Also, notice the form of the poem. I had fun playing around on the computer with line lengths and line breaks (called *enjambment*) trying to make the layout look like an animal neck yet still maintain the poem's natural order. Even when my artistic efforts don't quite come off, I can still have a fresh creative experience grappling with graphic design. My goal is to see or do something new every day as long as it is legal and moral. Well, at least legal. (Only kidding, Mom)

I have a poet friend who writes her verse in circles and all kinds of shapes. You often have to read her poetry upside down or back-wards while roaming around the page. Who says that poets are boring? Free-spirited freshness never ages or gets depressed. In an entirely different mood and for an entirely different purpose, I shaped my more serious poem, *Ground Zero*, to look like a missile.

AFRICAN ANIMAL

Palm tree by the pool
strutting giraffe neck
      lion mangy mane
     elephant skin
      date-tiger eyes
       monkey moves
        stares fiercely at me
         through the sand bars
          of my desert mirage zoo

LATE FOR WORK

Eight o'clock
Stayed-out-late midget pick-up
Eating doughnut going 60
Passes
Alarm-didn't-ring Honda Civic
Applying make-up doing 50

Like a wet dog after a bath
my car shudders
as each blurring vehicle
rockets around me

My computer mode mind
Set on critical
Clicks
Why don't they
Pay attention
Slow down
Quit...

My cell phone rings

READING FRIENDS

I sometimes choose friends
like a book—examine their cover,
see how they look—front, back,
and perfect bound spine.
Reading their pages
absorbed with each character
I linger with their laughter,
cry with their tears, fight
with their fears.

Like boring novels
we sometimes toss each other aside
on page 35.
But tested friendships,
rare and bound in real leather
line my permanent shelves
to be read and renewed.

TREE LOVE

The ice-winged Pine tree
Stands on a sea of snow

Reaching out to me
Bundled in my fir coat

I shake soggy flakes
From my limbs

Respond
With a melting embrace

Poets love to create a poem about creating a poem! It is also a keen way to live in the moment. Some of my own poetry speaks to the dilemma of finding that right word or original phrase that sets a poem apart from the singsong rhyming and clichés of the beginner. I may even moan in meter at not being able to bring forth a perfect poem. Writing about it is just another way of not taking ourselves so seriously. *Have fun* is what I tell all my workshop groups. Our goal is to enjoy the search and seizure of our creative voice as we bridge the gap between a bunch of words and a POEM.

Learning to paint images with words is an artistic experience—a brushstroke of ingenuity. It is also a musical moment because even free verse needs to have rhythm and music, but most of all it must speak TRUTH.

Many years ago I dabbled in interior design. I learned simple basic rules of color and pattern, how to arrange furniture and accessories, where to place pictures, as well as other aesthetic solutions without making a home look "decorated." To enter a room that I had "done" was to hopefully appreciate the entire effect without being aware of any of the rules or tools that I had used to achieve beauty and balance.

For me, poetry is somewhat like that. The craft should not be obvious even if a verse is metered or in rhyme. When I read someone else's creative work, I want to think, *Wow, I wish I had written that.* Clever use of words as well as a deep (or light-hearted) message speaks to me. The fun part of any creative writing is that we often write things we don't even know we know. That is why I've learned not to worry about writer's block. I find that when I really have something to say, it comes pouring out.

WRITER'S BLOCKETTE

Words squeeze
into stingy flow
like the last drops
of paint in a tube.
I look with lust at my
unabridged Webster
gyrating
thousands of word forms.
Why can't I fit them together
inside creative images
enjambing
them onto the page
with my poetry spray-gun?
Instead, I leave strokes
of dried up acrylic
with my mottled meter
paintbrush.
Heavy oil metaphors
choke my pen.
Lightweight alliteration
watercolors each stanza.

Oh epiphany, where art thou?

WEIGHTY WORDS

Obese words
waddle across the page.
My computer
pecks itself with black letters
meant to masticate into meaning,
losing weight of the unknown
with each idea transferred
into slim line font.
My muscular muse feeds me
a perfectly proportioned poem
with satisfying chunks of candor
that emerge from fat images
eating into my laptop.
I no longer
weight-watch each word.
My fully formed verse
awaits the critique.

POETRY OF LOVE

Love is my poetry
Life's
Alliteration

Metaphor magic
Miracle
Association

Making our connection
Shared
Repaired

Perennial seedlings
Flower
Together

In summer soil
Beneath
Rising stars

After becoming an "early widow" many years ago, the hardest thing for me was to be alone. Now with personal growth, I can honestly say that I love being and doing things by myself. Of course, I still enjoy my friends and spend time with them eating, going to events, and just plain "hanging out." I also truly love to be among strangers although I never think of them that way. My favorite hobby is to engage people whom I do not know in conversation. They always respond to some pleasantry (even in foreign countries) and as a result I have met amazing individuals, many actually becoming close long-term friends. Being alone has given me the freedom and opportunity to do this.

I also do a lot of my writing in restaurants. There is a Paris-like cafe in my hometown where I often eat breakfast and where much of my first book was written. The owners are family to me.

I have become such an independent cookie that I find I rebel at ritual. Not all, of course, but enough that I have changed many of my holiday habits. The complex meals and complicated arrangements as to who, what, where, and when just seemed unnecessary for me in my new life. So kudos to my understanding friends and family, I don't *have* to celebrate them any more! Lest you think, I am ungrateful or unpatriotic, I still love America but reserve my right under the constitution of the United States *not* to celebrate *every* holiday.

Maybe my sharing this can help other lonely or harassed souls realize that we really can make our own traditions which might be to do something special, to do nothing at all, or in my case write poems about *not* doing holidays. The following two poems are a composite of many tainted incidents.

21

I HATE HOLIDAYS

Not what they stand for,
just what they have become,
too much play-acting to the drama
of someone else's version of celebration.
Tradition is sort of doing the same thing
everyone else is doing, the same way
at the same time over and over again.

After one really grim Thanksgiving
I made the decision,
no more holidays—well, maybe one.
I do love the life of Jesus—rather the Christ,
the action of good. That used to be
what Christmas was about.
I can stand that.
Besides, I'd miss my family
if I were cruising Tahiti on the 25th of December.

Anyway, that stupid Thanksgiving
when I'm supposed to be feeling grateful,
I am listening to a boring cousin
stepping on the last line
of every story told by someone else—usually
with her own account of a similar circumstance
but not nearly as interesting as mine.
Our host hovers over the guests,
one of whom is asleep sitting straight up in his chair
and I am wondering how I can leave before dessert.
That was the last Thanksgiving I ever celebrated.
I am truly grateful to the pilgrims
for understanding.

WRITER'S THANKSGIVING

The only one in the Harbor Restaurant
alone.
Families interlacing around me
banter, borrow my chairs.

Now at a table for four,
three empty spaces,
I order
no turkey
no dressing
no cranberries.

Free
from shadowy ancestors
deciding
my holiday celebration
of mindless repetition,
steak please.

Is this a phase,
and one day I'll return
to the daze of cooking for hours,
eating in minutes?
Will my free full flower-hood
reverse to a root-bound robot seed?

A flowing stream of ideas
river-raft
through my sea of consciousness
docking at the pen in my hand
recording
satisfaction with solitude.

MOMENT OF TRUTH

Shedding my winter coat
Of worry

For the summer solace
Of serenity

The dark drizzle
Of anxiety

Opens to the skies
Of surprise

To receive the communion
Of epiphany

SCANNING BRIDGES

I spring forward
To the future
Cleats digging
Into the solid bridge of Now

I look back
Regret crossings fade
Directing my
New expansions

Ideas cantilever
Beneath social satellites
Art activates
Science connects

Humor unites
Poetry pacifies
Shaping my world
With bridges of choice

BRIDGES

TO THE

PAST

My Mid-western background is the subject of many of my poems. I have some fond (and not so fond) memories of growing up in a close farming community, an environment that gives me gentle soil in which to plant my poetry. These stories tell of a humble time in our national heritage, yet some of the innocence is overshadowed by an undercurrent of loneliness from the isolation of a farm and the nosiness of neighbors whose limited lives sometimes made them cross over the line of privacy.

I have actually used names of people I knew for my characters although some circumstances are imaginary. Lily and Harry Briscoe were my grand-parents, two sweet and supportive people in my life. I love writing from their perspective. I encourage you to write a few lines about your own childhood. It can be a healing and inspirational bridge to memories. You might be surprised at how kindly you remember the past, forgiving yourself and others.

When I give book talks, poetry readings, or workshops my audiences often include young people who have no personal knowledge of our country's life in the early to middle twentieth century. It is fun to hear their wonderment of my poems about the family farm. That time in our nation's history was full of life style simplicity, while at the same time it was also enormously complicated by having to maintain basic elements of food, shelter, and clothing, sometimes without electricity, indoor plumbing, telephones, or reliable transportation. Then, of course, there was life without television—unimaginable to my teenage listeners.

Rural Free Delivery, the subject of this next poem, was established in 1896 and became an important part of the postal system for a developing agricultural country.

RFD

I can hear him rattling down the road.
The wash sitting in the tin tub
ready to go through the wringer can wait.
Cows milked, animals fed,
but some things can just wait.
Poised for my run down the gravel drive
to the main road, I see dust in the distance.
I can usually gage my sprint
to be there the second
he stops his wheezing engine.
The flag is up—he has to stop.
Of course, I always put the flag up
so I can have at least one visitor a day.

I look across the field and see Briscoe
plowing the South forty—been at it since five.
Wish he'd look up so I could blow him a kiss.
He might even come running
if I waved an envelope.
Not that we expect anything important
except our Farmer's Almanac
is almost due.

It's time.
I wipe my hands on my faded floral apron
and race to the mailbox.
Freddy smiles as he cuts the motor.
He knew I'd be there.

Morning Lily.
Morning Freddy.
How was Charlie when you stopped
at his house?
Doing poorly, but his crops are in.
Will you tell Grace down the road, I'll see her
in town Saturday night?
Sure Lily. Here is a box from your sister
in California. Bet it's something pretty to wear.
The Parkers have a postcard from their son.
He says he got a new job and doesn't know when
he'll be back to see them. Hope that kid
appreciates his parents.
Me too, Freddy. Tell your Mae, hello.
O.K. Lily, see you tomorrow.

He waves across the field to Briscoe
and starts up his truck.
Conversation through the clatter
now impossible,
I walk back up the path
smiling for my second love,
Rural Free Delivery.

PARTY LINE

Two longs and a short,
the oak phone hanging on the kitchen wall
sings our special song.
Still amazes me that I can lift a handle
and hear people talk.

It's Nora Jane
wheedling help with the church supper
Sunday next.
Putting my mouth to the speaker
which sticks out like the spout on a teakettle,

I shout *yes* into its black hole
as if my words had to reach all the way to town.
Briscoe keeps telling me I don't have to yell.
*It's the wires on those poles
that carry the sound*, he says.

Nora Jane chats on,
her friendly gossip
soothes my aching loneliness
like liniment on a sore limb.
I love my telephone

its metal mouthpiece
magnifying neighbor news.
I hear a noise on the line.
Not me.
Not Nora Jane.

*Get off the phone, Mrs. Werner.
It's not your ring.*

CEMETERY COMPETITION

Memorial Day
was an enormous event in our tiny town.
We paraded
from downtown—eleven stores
to the cemetery—seven blocks.
We didn't know about floats
but we understood patriotism
waving our dime-store flags.
I even had red, white, and blue
crepe paper threaded through
the spokes of my bike
as I peddled the PARADE.

Everyone put fresh flowers
on the graves of their relatives.
Some ancestors went so far back
kin didn't seem to know whose they were
but I heard whispered names like
Uncle Charlie and Great-grandmother Lissie.
I thought you got some sort of prize
for the most flowers on the most graves.
After the cemetery celebration
we marched to the park for potluck
to stuff on Mom's fried chicken
and angel food cake.

I was back last summer.
The tombs still had flowers—few and fake,
heroes had flags—tattered and faded
but I wondered who they were for,
people who died
or the relatives who came and counted.

MY LAST DOLL

The last Christmas present under the tree,
Patsy Ann lies there
in the cellophane covered box,
a doll smile on her composition face.
Hair painted the color of almonds,
blue eyes that blink,
her arms and legs hang loosely
from a softly stuffed torso.

I gently hold my precious gift
in the crook of my arm
nursing her from my nine-year-old
breast-less chest,
just like Aunt Joanna.

Pristinely propped on pillows,
I only leave her to go to school.
She watches me grow
and outgrow,
stares at my skinned knees
then prom dresses
and dates.
Boyfriend after boyfriend
pour through the door
until finally we both know
this is the ONE.

She doesn't go on my honeymoon
but is the first
to be entertained in my new home.

She moves with us
from Illinois to Colorado
to New Mexico to Wyoming
to Arizona to California.
Last packed,
first unpacked,
her gaze never leaves me.

My new baby doll
really cries, really wets,
eats real food.
All the years of playing mother
give birth to reality.

Patsy Ann now watches
through the crack in the closet door.
First packed,
last unpacked.
Wrinkles and spots spread
like parched earth
over her face,
white dress yellows, blue eyes fade
living in a nursery of neglect.

Playing dress-up one day,
my daughter finds the play child
in its cardboard home on the shelf.
She gently holds my last doll
in the crook of her arm
as it nurses from her six-year-old
breast-less chest.

BURNING BRIDGES

I didn't mean
to light the spark of anger
that turned our relationship into flames
but I was burned.
All my life I have tried to please
with my good girl image
hoping to outgrow
your personified spoiled brat view.
I raised the bridge
so why can't you see the grown up me?

My letter tried to explain
but once a bridge starts to burn
even though it spans deep waters
there may be no bucket big enough
to squelch the blaze.

I watch from the bank
on my side of the river
as you stare across the chasm
making no attempt to
dampen the explosion.

I walk away
no smell of fire on my clothes.

I THOUGHT WE WERE RICH

We lived in the biggest house in town—
double story, walls twelve inches thick.
It even had two bathrooms.
None of the other seven hundred residents
in Westfield had two bathrooms—one up, one down.
Of course, there was no hot water heater
so we had to fire up the wood stove in the basement
for our Tuesday and Saturday baths.
Then, too, we didn't actually own the place,
more like, rented it for $25 a month.

My sister and I
were the best-dressed kids in school.
Our really rich cousins in California
sent us their barely-worn clothes
that almost didn't look like hand-me-downs.
One time my aunt hid a tiny gold locket
in among those like-new skirts and sweaters.

We also drove the only new Buick in town—
shiny black, white side walls.
My brothers took turns
washing it every Saturday
so they could drive it around the block.
Sometimes in summers
I got to go with my traveling salesman Dad
as he made calls all over the state of Illinois.

Even after I married the blond crewcut
with the blue convertible, the
I-thought-we-were-rich
stayed through the stage,
hope-we-make–it-to-the-next-paycheck.
 I was rich.

37

BUILDING

SOCIAL

BRIDGES

Social issues touch me dearly. The more I see my neighbor as a spiritual sibling living across the world as well as across the street, the more I want to right wrongs. Experience has taught me that helping others is actually helping our selves. It is like what the United States did after World War II with the Marshall Plan that helped rebuild Europe. History calls it *enlightened self-interest.* The results are obvious. It seems to be some kind of spiritual law that when we bless others, we are blessed as well— either from that same source or on an entirely different front.

Self-effacing social commentary is my favorite type of poetry, both to read and to write. We can say just about anything when we include ourselves in our critical observations about life on the daily scene. I do it rather easily since I have probably done (or thought about doing) many of the things that seem narrow-minded to me today.

Pointing fingers is a dangerous occupation. Poking fun is a sport. One of the things I find most distasteful is watching those with low self-esteem attempt to build themselves up by tearing someone else down. Probably the majority of criticism stems from that human failing.

No doubt the longest and steepest bridges we will ever cross are over our relationships with others. For many of us they span a lifetime of giving and receiving, as well as self-examination, self-sacrifice, and service,

This next section of poems deals with issues which we confront every day. Hopefully we can do it with a sense of empathy, a sense of justice, but most of all with a sense of humor.

41

SHOPPING CARTS

Self-help conveyers carry our lives,
groceries to the car, office supplies.

Children sit inside their moving jail,
grab things off the shelf, cry a mighty wail.

Home for the homeless, belongings in a bag
bulge through steel wires as wheels wobble and sag.

Why do some carts carol sad songs
composing their chorus of wrongs,

purring for the prosperous,
but creak off key at poverty?

POLITICAL CONVENTION

Spiels of the speaker
Invoke squeals from the congregation
Fists pound points
Words of evangelical manna
Echo through party cathedral
Absorbing new ancient message
Of a dozen messiahs

The process
Preaching to the converted
Concludes with
Famine of substance
Feast of balloons
Popping to the Beatitude
Happy Days Are Here Again

After the automobile accident that nearly took my life, I received a blood transfusion. Barely conscious of what was happening at the time, I realized even then, that blood does not make up who we really are. Later, reflecting upon my phantom donor, I knew that any lingering prejudices I may have had about class, color, or nationality were now dissolved.

We
Truly are
All
On the same
Bridge.

THE DONOR

I watch each drop of blood
crawl down the plastic tube
through a steel needle into my arm.

Whose ancestors are meeting mine
in this stream of life?
Is my neck turning red
from a rifle-toting, pick-up driving
macho male?
Do I now have the Latin blood
of a young mother
selling plasma to buy family food?
Will I be a new color—
shades of black, brown, yellow?

Is my donor an artist
or a farmer?
Will I have an urge to paint
or to plant?
Is he / she a PHD
or a high school drop out?

To whom do I owe my life?
Now that we have the same blood
are we kin?
Do we speak the same language,
have the same politics,
laugh at the same jokes?

As a pure
Daughter of the American Revolution,
am I being transfused
into a mixed-blood child of the Uni Verse,
the one song?

UNSTOPPABLE WOMAN

A dynamo dashing uphill,
momentum hurls ever upward.
Over mountains of mist
she keeps moving
leaping tall walls that would limit.
Swimming through rapids of doubt,
running from mediocrity,
self-reliant energy her
kilowatt to success.
No dormant days can discourage,
no power can dispossess.

Fear may come like a prowling tiger,
its glow-in-the-dark eyes
circle her campfire of content.
But smoking embers of confidence
bellow a breath
to rekindle the spark of
delight.

GLASS CEILING

Like the cover on a manhole
Masculine hands
Hold the lid
As I pound my fists on the glass ceiling

They see skirts
I see suits
When will the corporate coach
Pick me

Another *must-prove-myself* day
Run faster
Throw harder
Know more

To win the same game

Where were you on September 11, 2001? Who can forget? Whenever there is a national or world tragedy writing poetry about it helps me cope with the emotional outage—or outrage. I wondered why until I realized that putting thoughts on paper clarifies and purifies views. An open, fair-minded discussion with others might give perspective and peace on a subject, but nothing helps me more than solitary creative recording. I have found that drafting a poem will often bring a dimension, breadth and depth, to the experience that nothing else can.

Poets and Philosophers have been saying this for centuries. (Although I'd love to take the credit.)

William Wordsworth made the point perfectly, "Poetry is the spontaneous overflow of powerful feelings: it takes its origin from emotion recollected in tranquillity...."

"Poetry is nearer to vital truth than history", said Plato.

The English poet, Percy Shelly acknowledged that, "Poets are the unacknowledged legislators of the world."

This elegant definition of poetry came from Samuel Taylor Coleridge: "Poetry is the blossom and fragrance of all human knowledge, human thoughts, human passions, emotions, language."

Pretty heady stuff from rather good company, wouldn't you say? It is humbling for me to read quotes like these and realize that I am actually touching the fringes of such giants when I write the simplest of poems. And so can you, fellow poet.

After September 11, I immediately wrote the next poem, *Ground Zero.*

GROUND
ZERO

Twin trade towers
lanced by living missiles
of death into sixteen sad acres
smoking with hate rubble
fired by hearts in havoc
hiding egos of evil
in the guise of
worshipping
Allah
0

From the day after the attacks of September 11, 2001, I felt the pull of New York City from across the country. It was like a mother calling her family to come home saying, *your siblings are sick.* Finally six months after the attacks I was able to combine a trip to Ground Zero with attending a program sponsored by the United Nations honoring World Poetry Day.

My hotel was probably ninety blocks from the site but I felt the urge to walk. Taking a cab to such a shrine seemed obscene to me. After walking nearly forty-five blocks, I realized that my moral stand was beyond my physical stand. I found a cab but asked the driver (my new best friend created in the next forty blocks) to let me out far enough away so that I felt I was actually walking to my pilgrimage and not just being a tourist.

How does even a writer, a wordsmith, put the shrapnel of words together in order to describe such devastation? I know there have been grim scenes of obliteration throughout human history—whole cities, even whole countries—but until now, they have never been mine.

I walked part of the perimeter of the sixteen acres surprised at how empty the construction site or, in this case, the destruction site was beginning to look. Men and machinery were in motion yet a reverence filled the air even with the noise of orderly chaos.

No doubt everyone who witnessed the tragedy will have different reactions. My immediate emotion was shock at the senselessness and stupidity of such hate that would take so many innocent lives.

All I could think of was *BIG STUPID HOLE....*

BIG STUPID HOLE

They removed five more bodies
from the hole today,
six months, ten days, two hours later.
How different it looks standing here
from the pictures on my thirty-two inch TV.

Now the pit,
digesting and regurgitating
what it was forced-fed,
is across the street
not across the country.
I can't click it off
or hit instant replay
to reconstruct towers and revitalize lives.

I thought too, that New York City cops
would look, well, more cop-like.
But they look like me
or like my brother
or like my daughter
or like my neighbor's nephew.

This one, guarding
a missile-scarred American street,
is not even Irish.
His name tag says *Max Goldman*.
His uniform says *I am in charge*.
His eyes say *I am devastated*.
But he is alive,
gives me directions, smiles
Have a nice day.

I want to cry enough tears
to fill that big stupid hole.

WHITE HAT POET

I long to be a White Hat poet
to chase the Black Hats into the sea,
proclaiming verse that would reverse
the violence I see.

I hope my White Hat poems
unwind a black turban or two
turning it white with insight,
then rewind with what's right.

Maybe my White Hat muse
will remove a burka or two
whose honeycomb slotted view
hides an unheard female voice,
then I'd like to cover her up
with poetic veils of her choice.

Could my White Hat prose
topple a black Stetson or two,
make every CEO write a poem
about what he plans to do?

I want simple White Hat rhyme
to build strong ties that bind,
exchange ideas, expunge lies,
all in the name of the good guys.

I long to be a White Hat poet
healing wounds with words,
uniting in you and me
a brotherhood that stood
and chased the Black Hats into the sea.

RISE AND FALL OF AN IDEA

New Truth initiates a crusade parade

Loyal bands
Theme floats
Line up behind Leaders
Who promote the Cause
Protect the idea
Orchestrate red taped routes

Adherents assemble
Honor their Grand Marshall
Sing praises to progress

Officers-in-charge
Write rules
Mark boundaries
Build concrete barriers
Arrange converts in
Committee formation

Storms begin to build
Floats break down
Bands play off key
Banners fall
Marchers stumble
Structures crumble
Idea
Crushed

Down the road another parade is forming

DOT.COM OFF-RAMP

High-tech teen
drives his computer
on the super-highway of the universe,
speeding across a color screen.

Which lane to choose?
Fast or slow?
Parental signals
flash red and green
in his megabyte mind.
Ideas collide.

Accelerating on the web,
he rides the freeway
to infinite information.
Green light.

He brakes at porno e-mail—
dead-end road.
Red light.

Do years of love and supervision
make the decision?

BLAME

Always just a hair away
    Accusing
        Explaining
            Justifying

Every act or accident
    Finger points
        Your fault
            My fault

Blame needs no name

COCKTAIL PARTY PARASITE

Vodka in hand
she walks across the room,
black stiletto heels
elevating her
one step above a pigmy.

Penetrating our cozy conversation,
her cutting critique
impales the females
to imaginary rival stakes
with back-stabbing grace.

Nauseous innuendo
meant to maim, ricochets,
slashing her own widget wrists.
I step over slain egos
and move on.

OUT OF THE ENVELOPE

Explodes a seventy-year-old secret
How many sleepless nights
Composed Uncle Tim's letter

Mailed to every niece and nephew
Because one new-to-the-family
Asked *why have you never married*

No meanness
No giggle behind her hand
Only innocent interest

The rest of us
In our polite sophistication
Never asked

We wondered
We whispered
We wisened

I shed a silent tear
For this sad hermit
Writing genius poeting loneliness

Gay peg
In a straight-peg world
That denies the differences among us

Giving no place at its family table
With too many hushed names
And empty chairs

I have mixed emotions about the death penalty because I know that taking a life does not bring back a life. I have switched sides several times on this issue and no doubt will again as I gain new views. The day that Timothy McVeigh was killed by lethal injection for the Oklahoma bombing in the United States, this poem wrote itself with my pen.

It expresses what I pray happened the moment that Timothy received the fatal injection and crossed life's final bridge—hopefully from hate to remorse to love.

REMORSE INJECTION

He looks around
his lethal chamber
watching himself
being unstrapped.
Rising
effortlessly
wordlessly
Timothy moves across
the field of 168 chairs
holding each hand
and whispering,
Will you forgive me?
168 echoes.
I forgive you.

How many times have we relived the past with the mantra "if only I...," or "why didn't I...?" Of course, we can't go back to that lost moment but perhaps writing about the experience in an in-depth, analytical, and forgiving way can bring us peace from regrets and guilt.

Writing a letter to someone who hurt us or angered us can actually stop the inner chatter of all the brilliant things we wish we had said but didn't. We may never send that letter or even know to whom to address it, but putting collected thoughts on paper brings closure to the unrest. That is why I always find composing poetry to be a healing remedy that can crystallize jumbled thinking.

The following poem is an example of how venting poetically about an experience that had bothered me for years has now stopped the rehearsal of mental images about what I should have done. I have finally been able to let it go with a prayer and a poem.

Abused children around the world continue to be an unacceptable social scourge. Poetry has made me more socially aware and has given me a bridge to express my concerns and hopefully know what to do. Throughout history that has been the role of writers so we are in good company when we challenge in-justice wherever we see it.

WHAT SHOULD I DO?

When they enter the ice cream store
I feel their meanness
like rabid dogs on attack,
a stringy-haired grandmother
with two teen-age girls.
Cowering behind them
a six-year-old boy
holds a penny sucker in dirty hands.

The sisters order double scoops in waffle cones,
their little brother—nothing.
As they talk and laugh
the child sitting on skinny knees
whimpers, his frantic eyes glazed
with the oblivion of neglect
lock on the luxurious treat.
Ignored
until one of the girls turns,
venom violating her voice,
What are you staring at?

My daughter and I exchange silent censure.
I watch my own grandchildren
licking their chocolate cones
securely fastened in love.

What should I do?

Years later that terrified child face
still haunts me.
Why didn't I...
If only I had...
I pray.

Society is also becoming more aware of the problems of both mental and physical spousal abuse. When I write poems with a social message, I try to understand what the victims involved might be feeling. Never having been physically abused myself I don't know how such violence feels but, like most of us, I have taken some measure of mental abuse. I wrote the next poem from a totally imaginary point of view. From research I have learned a great deal about how the controller / abuser operates with repeated cycles of charm, cruelty, and repentance. Then more charm, more cruelty, and finally more repentance...until....

The one being continually abused will usually develop a diminished sense of self, which the small personal pronoun "i" might indicate in a poem. Contemporary poets will often use that tool to make a point or get a particular mood across. I am told that English is one of the few languages which enhances the ego with a capital "I." Most other languages use a small "i" in a sentence other than at the beginning.

Even words can wound...

WOUNDED WORDS

i fall over your sharp words
cutting me like ragged rocks
on the beach

lunging lizard
acid tongue
burns through my thin skin
leaking tears

until
after
your soft somnolent sounds
bandage my wounds

i forgive
again

When a friend made a major move, the movers broke the leg of her antique dining table. A craftsman was sent to repair it. He gently glued, sanded, stabilized, and stained for hours, singing to himself. After he was finished, my friend looked at the results and exclaimed *why it looks as good as new!* The craftsman grinned and replied *no Mrs. Gladden it's better than new.*

She could see that all the time and effort, expertise and joy he had cemented into repairing her wooden table had made it sturdier than before. For me, that simple experience of my friend's has become a metaphor for meeting challenges and coming away stronger than ever—and doing it with a song!

I had tried and tried to put that epiphany into a poem but I wasn't satisfied with the results until I finally wrote two poems with the same title—one free verse and one prose poem. It became my experience.

Now will you try to put this same story into a poem of some sort?

BETTER THAN NEW

Broken table
Broken promises
Broken relationships

Decision the same
Do I fix it
Do I toss it

Self-repairs
Represent investment
Days months years

My reward
As good as new
BETTER THAN NEW

BETTER THAN NEW

I watch him fix it—gluing, sanding, staining—singing all the while. My mother-in-law would die a second death if she knew—her antique dining table limping on a broken leg. She would probably look at it like a racehorse that needed to be shot but I am determined to at least try to save my inheritance from the glue factory for dead antiques.

Finally finished, the craftsman silently pleads for my approval. I can't find even the tiniest hairline crack. I wow my praise. *It's as good as new! No,* he says, *it is better than new.*

OK, so I start fixing every break in my life *and* with a song. What do you know? *Better than new.*

65

GAMES

OF

BRIDGE

Crossing bridges can become a game of scrabble when you finally find your poetic voice to sing (or scream) your feelings. Poetry critique groups and workshops teach me a great deal. If you have one in your area and are serious about writing, you might want to check it out. Pour your pride in a bottle and leave it in the car because it will be tough to take the criticism if your don't. Having another poet critique your poetry is like someone criticizing your child. *How dare they!* But sometimes even our children benefit from the objective view of someone else. The opinion of peers can be immensely helpful. We don't need to agree or accept their advice, but as far as poetry goes, if they are experienced poets then we had better swallow hard, breathe deeply, and take it. They do have to be kind, supportive, and fun—or find another group.

Writing exercises are a terrific way to express originality. One of the cleverest and most enjoyable workouts for me is to write a poem incorporating seven or eight words selected by a member of the group. Everyone uses the same words in any form and the variety of verse released from such a creative process is unbelievable. Unusual word combinations magically appear on the page. It is proof to me of our individuality and uniqueness.

I used this method in the following four poems. Notice that the first two contain seven of the same words as well as a similar theme but one is a parody on the other. They were especially satisfying to explore because I was able to use a literary device and make a social statement at the same time. This section includes a few more tools of the craft that have helped me to promote my own poetic progress.

69

INDIAN MAIDEN

<u>Bored</u>, she sits by the steamy springs
<u>sipping</u> water from a hollow yellow <u>gourd</u>,
her bare Indian legs
<u>swoop</u> in and out of the *agua caliente*.
Laying the <u>container</u> on the silent sand
she removes a pink shell comb
with its <u>nine</u> sharp teeth
from the leather pouch around her neck.
Hair perfectly <u>parted</u>, she begins braiding
the waist-length black silk.
Warm water and sympathetic sun
bathe her being.

INDIAN SQUAW

Bored, she slumps over the steamy bar
in the Agua Caliente Casino
sipping vodka from a gourd-shaped glass,
her ancient Indian legs wrapped
around a wooden stool.
Parted-in-the-middle waist-length gray hair
barely contained by an elastic band.
She swoops her last nine dollars
out of the plastic purse swinging on her arm
and heads for the slot machines.
Neon lights and liquor glow
bathe her being.

JUST ANOTHER K*

My blue planet
hums around the sun,
sponging
another millennium.
Faucet of fears
running neck and neck
join the science of technology
creaking its way to twenty K

(sponge, twenty, neck, science, creaky, hum, join,
faucet)

*Written in 1999 just before the turn of the century.

SUNDAY SERMON

Standing in the sun-lit pulpit,
the preacher drones
as he drives his devil message
down the evangelical road
filled with chuck-holes of fear.
I huddle against my Mother
on the hard pine pew,
her scent of freshly baked bread
singing to me
as I pick the scab
off the sore on my shin
and watch a column of blood trickle
onto my white sock.

Suddenly Reverend George
flails his hands heavenward
like a maestro
conducting a faltering orchestra.
The veins on his persimmon neck
protrude as if they were
mole tunnels in clay soil.

Cease ye from sin, you sinners.

The congregation stirs,
preening ruffled feathers
while guilty *amens* seep from blank lips.
My mother encircles me with angel arms
that silently say,
He's not talking about us.

(ruffle, cease, column, shin, bread, you, blank)

I have become a cheerleader for poetry. There seems to be a renaissance of this artistic medium invading the country. Or maybe it appears that way to me because I have just discovered the New World of Poetry and imagine poets landing on every shore. However, when the Poet Laureate of the United States regularly reads his poetry on a national news show then there must be somewhat of an awakening of the masses—like me.

Young people usually love to write poetry. So I have begun volunteering in our local schools helping to teach students the craft as well as encouraging an appreciation for what writing poetry can do for their emotional health and self-confidence. I use myself as an example. Teenagers can't argue with someone who has a whole new fabulous life from learning to express herself through the genre of poetry.

One of the assignments I give students in order to bring out their talent and originality is to write from the standpoint of an inanimate object. Of course, I have to practice what I preach (don't you hate that?) so I am including one of my poems written as a *thing*. If you don't know what I am in the first version of *Born to Fly* (next page) then I didn't do it right.

On occasions when I perform my poetry with harp or piano, I change the pronoun from *me* to *she,* as I did in the second version. Both of the renditions are included here to show how simple it is to take a poem and convert it into a whole different voice and layout.

BORN TO FLY

Covered in spangles of stars and strips
My skirt swirling in red, white, and blue,
I bear the banner of law
At liberty to fly as high as a New York sky.
Reflected in the eye of every American,
I look up to the sun—out from the moon.
Burned with hate I perish for freedom.
The national anthem makes me stand tall
Yet I barely crawl halfway up the mast
For heroic death.
Size-wise I am small,
Symbol-wise I am infinite.
I wave forever
Even, when no one waves back.

BORN TO FLY

Covered in spangles of stars and strips,
skirt swirling in red, white, and blue,
our flag bears the banner of law
at liberty to fly as high as a New York sky.
Reflected in the eye of every American,
she looks up to the sun—out from the moon.
Burned with hate, perishing for freedom,
the national anthem makes her stand tall
yet barely crawl halfway up the mast
for heroic death.
Size-wise she is small,
symbol-wise she is infinite
waving forever,
even when no one waves back.

Another clever trigger for creating a poem is to use sound as the underlying theme like this next one, *After the Funeral.* When I took a writer's workshop at Indiana University the instructor asked the class to compose a verse describing sound of some sort. It is amazing to me that we can reach into our memory bank for something as simple as noise and withdraw an experience from a past deposit that happened to us years before.

I had forgotten this emotional moment until I was forced to bring it into such an unusual kind of literary structure. Writing about it helped me to see how far I have come since that sad day. I was able to describe a devastating moment in my life without grief.

When I had finished the assignment I also realized that although the ticking clock was the catalyst for the poem other sounds blared out as well—the click of the lock, squeaking leather, singing wings—even silence. Doesn't it show how you never know what magic metaphor lurks inside your poetry engine ready to ignite the spark of epiphany?

I kid you not,
this is thrilling stuff.

AFTER THE FUNERAL

Closing our front door
clicks a punctuation point of finality.
The ticking clock
metronomes a chore now mine,
once-a-week winding
the antique masterpiece.
How many times
we laughed our private joke—
his one sweep at housekeeping.

I plunge into the worn brown chair,
a leather nest
sized for his six-foot frame.
My five-feet-seven inches squeak perfectly
into its mellow hollows.

The husband chair
wraps his feather cushions around me
like singing dove wings
protecting their young,
yet prepared to release me
to silently fly alone.

A useful exercise that helps prime the mental pump to release the flow of ideas is called "stream of consciousness" recording. Writing continuously for several minutes about whatever comes to thought, letting it pour out onto paper (or computer) is a free-spirited adventure in self-discovery. This type of writing abandon is even considered by some to be cleansing therapy—an opportunity to wash away unwanted negative residue and possibly turn it into the positive vehicle of poetry.

Sometimes we surprise ourselves and bring forth a whole poem. Other times the effort might provide original metaphors, innovative imagery, and novel word medleys.

The following prose poem recalled from my teenage years is the result of using that process. I usually edit all my work many times after the first draft but this one pretty much stood without change. It is so "not me" that no one recognized it as mine when it was pulled from the pile and read at our poetry critique group. Part of the creative process is to do something that is like nothing we have ever done before—a sparkling new bridge.

Actually,
that pretty much describes
my whole approach
to life!

NOSES

When I was a teenager I was sitting in the back seat of a car with a bunch of my friends playing a ukulele when the driver turned around to say some smart-ass thing about my playing. At that moment we went off the country road and into a ditch.

The stupid instrument came up and hit me in the face nearly cutting off my nose. A farmer took us to a hospital. Fortunately for me there was a doctor on duty who had just returned from the war. He had learned plastic surgery in England, so in that tiny, wood-shingled hospital he sewed my nose back into place.

I had to breathe out of my mouth for a few days but after the stitches were taken out it was nose as usual. It took a long time for that red scar to fade but I rubbed cocoa butter on it like our family physician said. Boy, did I feel ugly!

I became conscious of every passing nose. Noses became news to me. I never noticed how they don't always fit the face. I knew there were big ones but I never realized how small a nose could be. I also wondered if smells were different depending on the size variation.

I watched nostrils flare, dance, wiggle, wheeze, drip. Noses were straight and as long as a football field or curved like a racetrack. Some leaned right, some left. Some turned up, some down. They had hickeys, moles, warts, and hair covering young to old noses. The only nose I couldn't look at was my own.

Now pretend you are a poet. Pick a subject such as some remembered drama in your life or even a mundane event that you may be looking at in a whole new way. If you are a total beginner just record anything to get thoughts on paper. Don't worry about rules, tools, or technique—even syntax or spelling. You can always tighten your poem later. As you poetize you will become aware of telling your story with clarity, economy of language, rhythmic line breaks, and most of all—HAPPINESS.

Maybe it would help to know more about how a poem is edited so that you won't feel discouraged with your first draft. In editing the following poem, *Miss Alice*, I considered eliminating the last two lines because the ending couplet tends to summarize rather than show a poetic point. When it comes to poetry the rule is SHOW, don't TELL. (Use imagery to show an emotion or idea and not just tell about it.) But I decided to keep those two punch lines because I felt that they convey what the poem is really all about—a life changing experience at six! What would you do?

Notice, too, that I used the title as the first line of the poem so in this case the next line needs no capitalization. These are personal choices and small refinements that help create structure and form. The more you read contemporary poetry the more you will see that punctuation and capitalization use are changing all the time. The poet, e.e. cummings rewrote many poetry paradigms with his unusual style (even his name). I am experimenting all over the place myself. Read your composition out loud and you will hear things that you didn't see. Just start over that unexplored, uncharted bridge of self-expression and ENJOY!

MISS ALICE

stared at me sternly.
Come here at once Dessa Lee Byrd.
I must have done something awful
to be called by my whole name.

I trembled in front of her desk
as she took the hated RULER
from the left-hand drawer.
We never actually measured anything
with that piece of pine,
except maybe our badness.

Hold out your hand,
she ordered.
All the six-year-old eyes watched,
wide with horror—or happiness,
depending on how well they liked me.
As she smacked my pencil-holding palm
I wished I had held out the other.

The sting on my hand lasted an hour.
The sting on my heart lasted a lifetime.

BRIDGES

TO

TRAVEL

Travel provides miles of material for creating poetry, probably because it forces us over foreign bridges. Wandering the world or even exploring our own community can often give us the inspiration and the motivation to record new experiences in our journals, or on a paper napkin, for that matter.

Since I am such a social creature, I talk to just about everyone who comes within a two-foot radius. Consequently, I meet delightful and extraordinary people. They often become friends whom I learn something from and sometimes end up being the incentive for a poem or an essay.

On a visit to The Metropolitan Museum of Art in New York City I was looking at one of my favorite paintings of the bridge over Monet's lily pond. I told the lady standing next to me that I had actually stood on that bridge in his garden in France. She seemed pleased that I would speak to her. She was from Russia and eagerly shared information about museums in her country. Shortly after we parted she returned with a postcard that she had purchased for me from the museum's gift shop. It had a print of the painting we had just been admiring. I was so touched that I was speechless. (Well, maybe not completely.) I quickly looked to see how I could reciprocate and found a small flyer in my purse with two of my poems printed on it that I gave to her. We each signed our gifts and parted with a hug. My new best friend for seven minutes.

Only in America, you say? Many countries actually, since I have had similar encounters around the world.

MONET

I live in every painting

I am Camille posing in a field
my white dress blowing
in the Normandy breeze
I hide in each wheat stack
season to season
I am a bee buzzing water lilies
that float on his Oriental pond
Sitting inside the fog fretted cathedral
I seek conversion
As I stand in the station
steam from a train
veils my face

Every place there is a Monet
there is a me

PARIS POETRY READING

He shuffles into the seedy room
that calls itself a trendy bookstore café.
I watch our nursing-home refugee
settle into a fragile folding chair.
Eyelids droop,
chin lounges on his tattered tweed coat
as he sits motionless
like a stray dog in front of a warm fire.

A glowing introduction
beams on this icon of poetry.
Our listless laureate leaps to perform,
forty years fall at his feet.
French verse dancing,
ideas transcending language
crackle from his tissue paper lips.
Eyes shine like spotlights on a stage.

Poetry licks the audience
with its silky tongue
while aging muse becomes
Lord of the metaphor.

ALTA'S COFFEEHOUSE AT THE BEACH

The Local's hangout,
its cement floor and garage sale chairs
gathered around chipped teeth tables,
a refrigerator magnet
for culture and counter-culture.
Colored flyers like flags from a ship
wave on a bulletin board harboring
poetry readings, soul music.

I watch.

Lovers huddle in a corner
lighting love fires
with their match stick touch.
Beach bum from Beverly Hills
wearing silk warm-up
and Gucci tennis shoes,
greets her cheek-touching friend.
A cell phone sings *Hail to the Chief.*
An obvious want-a-be answers,
scanning his audience
for the properly impressed.

I'm not.

Retirees hobble in, grab
personalized mugs
off the rack on the wall,
settle around the window table
to rehearse a grocery list of ailments
bought into a thousand times
as their political commentary
sucks up the air.

I leave.

88

VIEW FROM THE RITZ

Ascending the mini-mountain
my car purrs with pleasure
anticipating its destination
of elegant association,
Rolls and Mercedes—
perhaps jock with a Jag.

Breakfast on the patio
reveals a view of the valley
ordained by the sun,
expansive, expensive.
Familiar landmarks
poke through palms like fronds.
Sprinklers on a hundred golf courses
mist the desert floor
with tiny rainbows.
Mountains, colorful and moving
as an Indian dance, circle the horizon.

Attache cases open,
faces tense,
business men pontificate
into cell phones
while a honeymoon couple
see only the scenery of one another.
A little boy stares at his pancakes,
syrup scrolling down skinny arms
as his nanny, speaking gently,
directs, corrects.

The chorus of servers
chant the Ritz refrain,
My pleasure, my pleasure.

INERTIA

Living
In the safe harbor
Of sameness
Land-locks
Change
Anchors adventure
Resists sailing
Into an unknown sea

DREAM TRAVEL

Night sounds resisting
day rounds
push and pull me
like licorice taffy
sticking to my faded dream.

I climb onto the four A M train
traveling
East—or West
following parallel lines to a new Now
without name.

In my sleep-wake
I navigate the dining car
wishing I had brought a robe,
navy nightgown and bare feet
scream dream to elegant Orient Express stares.

A white-coated waiter
speaking Russian,
serves me caviar and crackers
on Czar studded china plates.
I thank him in Russian!

Staring out the window
as our black bullet
tunnels through the arctic tundra
I translate my dream journey
continents away from my bed.

SPIRITUAL

BRIDGE

The stage play of personal disaster usually gets our attention in a hurry. Nothing turns us to God or whatever we call a Higher Power like misfortune. I have had several major upsets in my life so as a young woman I was compelled to choose a spiritual path. A solid foundation was laid for the expectancy of good over evil no matter what the circumstance. That reliance has been my salvation ever since. Therefore, in 1997, after I suffered a life threatening auto accident I knew that my sustaining strength was in feeling the presence of God, the law of good.

When I first began to jot down some of my insights during months of recovery, the ideas were almost always of a spiritual nature. Putting on paper what I considered "truths" made them seem more real and powerful to me—a healing exercise.

Gradually it grew therapeutic to write about the world around me, both real and imaginary. I began to be more attentive to my surroundings. That is when my musing turned to poetry. I viewed things from a whole new perspective and recorded my observations in verse. The light turned on and love for my new Mother Tongue has never dimmed. For me to be able to say in a few choice words what otherwise might have taken pages to express is an exploration equal to landing on the moon. It has metaphorically been ONE GIANT STEP FOR DESSA.

I hope your poetic steps can be as healing and as much fun as my voyage has been. The Bible is full of insightful men and women who articulated their love for God and man through the imagery of poetry.

So can we!

*I AND MY FATHER ARE ONE**

One like rays to the sun
One like branches from a tree
One like waves by the sea
One like grains in the sand
One like fingers on my hand

Not the same
But one
Like Father
Like son

*John 10:30

WHO? ME?

From Genesis to Revelation
God speaks—or shouts softly,
Go. Do. Lead. Heal.

Abraham laughed, Moses argued,
Jonah fled, Peter denied, Thomas doubted.
Yet, in the end,
overcoming self and separation,
they went, they did, they led, they healed
and became our inspiration.

When divine direction knocks at my door,
will I laugh, argue, flee, deny, doubt?
If I surrender to the Psalm,
Whither shall I go from thy spirit?
or whither shall I flee from thy presence?
and the words of Jesus,
I can of mine own self do nothing...
the Father that dwelleth in me,
he doeth the works,
then my, *Who? Me?*
may hear, *No. Us.*

Psalms 139
John 5, 14

AMERICA PRAYS

I hear America praying and listen to what she is saying. The flaming pictures of horror light paths for her warriors as prayers reveal solutions that heal. I *feel* America praying and thank God for what she is saying.

INNER CONNECTION

Connected to our Parent Source
Spiritual siblings touch
Like points on a star
Perpetually rolling through
Infinity together
Sisters supported
Brothers united
Aligned
In our mutual
Planetary purpose
I cut my hand
Humanity bleeds
Our interwoven lives
Weave a tapestry
Of universal family
Burning candles of brotherhood
Lighting the constellations

LANGUAGE OF LOVE

The language of Love *speaks* no terrorism
    Recites boundless words for heroism

The language of Love *leaps* to our lips
    Prayers that resolve angry conflicts

The language of Love *sweeps* a sunbeam
    Powers a rushing mountain stream

The language of Love *creeps* or it crawls
    Blesses where it lifts and where it falls

The language of Love *reaps* a faith
    Rebukes translation to hate

GIFTS OF CHRISTMAS

*

The
hands
of Love
reach out
like the Magi
bearing holy gifts
to the Christ Child
swaddled in goodness
I receive His love wrapped
without strings packaged in
glittering glory
forever

SHADOW OF LOVE

I feel the gentle flutter
of heart wings
flying on laugh lines in my face
breathing
a silent salute
to your presence

Long gone
in ashes of death
blown to sea
with sorrow
I will always feel your shadow
my one love

Too early
for a last journey
at the noon of your manhood
crossing waves of living light
launched on an infinite voyage
through eternal Life

NEW MOTHER

Madelynn Marie
Alliteration
Of love
Giving birth to your life
Added worth
To mine
Where have you been
Little girl
A being like yours
Must always
Have lived
Part of the eternal plan
To be my child
Never made
By time
Whose life
Have you blessed
Before mine
Held as a glint
In the Eye of God
You glisten
In the eyes of your mother

EMAIL PROPAGANDA

I recognize the screen name.
Subject: *Patriotic Greeting.*
All the forwards must have
traveled the globe at least twice.

Bit-by-bit the blue screen
transforms into a smiling six-year-old boy
standing at attention,
hand clutching a tiny American flag.
He shoulders a toy rifle,
cork connected by six-inch cord,
plugged in its barrel.

Tears attack my eyes
witnessing a child mimic patriotism—
playing war,
innocent target to an unknown enemy.

How I would love to take that cork,
plug every shotgun
that ever killed a living thing,
plug every semiautomatic
that ever gunned down
students as they walked to class,
plug every hidden handgun
that ever robbed a Seven Eleven,
plug every rifle of any caliber
that shot its way to sniper fame,
plug every missile and dumb smart bomb
computer guided
to a village or hut or city apartment
anywhere in the world.

But most of all I want to put a cork
on every radical group and politician
in every country
that espouses war,
exports terrorism
preaching that peace comes purely
by killing your opponent.

I know of only one cork big enough to plug
all the holes in the universe,
*_Our Father which art in Heaven_
Hallowed be Thy name....

---

*This may be my solution to reduce global evil but what about yours? Why don't you rewrite the last two lines to express your own view? That will make you a poet with a voice.

I almost did not include the following poem of four couplets in this new collection because of its simplistic form and contrived rhyming scheme. I can admit that now because I have learned (pretty much) to understand and appreciate well-crafted poetry. However, since its spiritual message was especially helpful to me during the months of my recovery and when journalizing my deepest insights was absolutely essential in crossing a healing bridge, I decided to share this early poem.

Perhaps it will help others realize that their own fledgling attempt at writing doesn't need to be great poetry to be helpful and healing. As I've grown in the art of creating poems, I have endeavored to improve my style while still capturing the insight. As one reviewer commented about my first poetry / self-help book, "She has written simple poetry with a profound message." That is still my goal.

PURITY

Love is God's purest form
No place for evil born

Or mortality's strife
In spiritual life

Nothing in Being to harm
Nor cause me to feel alarm

My substance is pure as my Source
Impelled by one powerful Force

Teaching Sunday School is one of the joys of my life. Children are natural poets because they have almost no inhibitions. After we study the Bible Lesson for the current week my class will often craft what they have learned into a poem. Sometimes we do it together chasing ideas like hide-and-seek and call it poetry tag. There are times when the students like to write spiritual summaries in poetry on their own, huddled over colored paper, hiding their work to surprise me.

What they compose is truly amazing. Writing in verse gives them spiritual stature and esteem as well as an appreciation for what they are learning about their relationship with God.

These budding poets often plant brilliant seeds in the soil of my poetry garden and later I will sprout a poem from something they have taught me!

With their permission, I am including two of their poems.

SAPPHIRE GLORY

The universe
is made of
bright blue sapphire
thoughts
that sparkle and shine
like the glory of God
with power to be All-in-all

Brittany de Coster
Age 11

I AM THANKFUL

The understanding of God
Makes me safe
The love of my Mom and Dad
Makes me safe
Going to Sunday School
Makes me safe
The safety and love of God
Makes me happy

Annette Marvin
Age 7

SILLY BRIDGES

I HAVE

CROSSED

Don't be afraid to think and write your nutty thoughts. You may not want to show your work to anyone but, then again, you might find an audience for your crazy poems or short stories. I have. Most people love humor—even silly. Such wit can heal hidden fears, annoyances, and lack of confidence as well as take away self-inflicted stress. Funny is fun and can often be a healing bridge to something or to someone, somewhere. I have read where medical research is finding that laughter actually is good medicine.

It sure works for me. When life seems dark, the absurd usually kicks in. It has been my amazing grace through most of my life. Even from a hospital bed after the automobile accident that turned me into a born-again poet my first words to a visitor were, *we have got to quit meeting like this.* A cliché, of course, but can't you image how comforting that was for my family—and me?

That is why even my more serious poems hopefully have a light touch. Sadness does not heal but joy does. Maybe that is why I get along so well with young people. Once when I was cutting up with a high school class while teaching them to appreciate and write poetry I said, *I love you all because you are so weird.* A young man in the back of the room called out, *and that's why we love you—you are so weird.* It was probably my greatest compliment from a teenager.

OK, it is your turn.
Think weird!
Write eloquently.

113

LINE DANCING AT THE BANK

We wait

Right foot stance
Left foot hold
Sighs
Twirling eyes
Shuffle

Teller calls
One step forward

We wait

BABBLE

I know he wants to watch the game
Yet I babble
Tired of his silent sounds
I babble
Competing with pigskin
I babble

Throwing the ball
Into his court of conversation
He dribbles a response
I know
I am out of bounds
Yet
I
Just
Keep
Babbling

One day while using a salt shaker, I began to wonder how life would look from the weighty world of the glass containers in my hand. Putting life and emotions into inanimate objects can give birth to unbelievable (and believable) originality. It is just plain fun to think in ridiculous terms. Who would imagine salt and pepper competing for attention?

I can.
Now *you* can.

SALT SEGREGATION

Why can't I be alone?
Why am I always paired
with this course ebony flake
whose dark good looks attract?
Just once,
I would like to stand on my own,
in my virginal white,
single and separate.

My subtle mission
brings out the best in every contact,
enhancing the palate.
Pepper's condiment competition
is an obvious ploy
for some spice in life.

His glass house is identical to mine.
That mysterious macho attitude
just makes it look more impressive.
At least I command top billing.
I am always picked first.

I'm sure some of my friends will be surprised at the next poem since it is not my usual style. I wrote it in jest. Humor that shocks especially self-effacing humor can often help lighten the load when we need to cross over an insecure bridge.

I don't usually like offensive words in writing or in speaking, for that matter, but occasionally an obscenity will make a point in poetry that nothing else can. "Truth in poetry" requires colorful even vulgar language sometimes since it is so much a part of contemporary society.

When I started writing this poem, I had not intended for it to rhyme but frequently a poem takes on a life of its own and does exactly what it wants to do. That is what this one did. It has several rhyming schemes, with both inner rhyme and end rhyme. All are acceptable although many poets believe that if you set a definite pattern of rhyming in the beginning, it is better to stick with it throughout the poem. *Bitter Sweet* has no pattern at all and that is OK too.

BITTER SWEET

Sometimes it feels downright sticky
to be nice all the time.
I do love the sweetness of sugar
but occasionally
I replace my sweet tooth with spice.

Once, when driving with friends
each out-impressing the other,
I replied with marshmallow innocence,
Really? No shit!
Several off-ramps later
they finally stopped laughing a bit.

Used to divinity in my nature,
obscenities dipped and delivered
with dark chocolate complexion
not the expected confection.

If I chose those words every day
from my box of bitter sweets
I'd boil just another batch of foul fudge,
yet every assortment of treats
needs at least one naughty nutty nudge.

MATRON'S MARATHON

Two hundred pounds
weighted by too many pieces
of too many pies
pound the pavement,
sweat squiggling down
her mirrored sunglasses
like water on a windshield.
She wipes her face on
the free red T-shirt
advertising this year's
marathon for fat females.
Losing the lead
she retreats to last,
too embarrassed
to win, place,
and especially show.

I LOVE WORMS

Maybe I love them because I know how much my garden loves worms. Before I became an adult, "yuck" was my term for a worm.

This morning after a desert rain, there was a worm working its way through muddy ground onto my slippery ceramic tile. When I say working I mean *working*. I wanted to charge in and help him / her make the big leap. I also felt I needed to instruct him / her on worm rules, number one is *stay out of the sun*. Even #30 sun block would not keep this gooey child of worm motherhood from drying out and becoming a stiff stick to be hosed off my patio.

What I truly learned today while watching my new worm best friend, was how brilliantly he made his moves across a diamond world. Like a baseball player, he slid onward with endless enthusiasm and determination to cover all the bases. With each forward play he grew, and he grew, and he grew. My shiny worm looked just like a greased little leaguer waiting for the pitch until he stretched his full length. Then he became a major league hitter and increased four inches in the process of running for home.

Moral: Keep moving around every obstacle no matter how hard (or soft) and you win the World Series. Don't stop even if you're out of your league. Besides, a Cardinal or an Oriole might eat you for a Giant lunch and you will end up with the Angels.

Now if I can just love these ants crawling up my leg....

**WHAT CAN I SAY?
IF YOU DON'T GET
THE FOLLOWING POEM
YOU'RE DEAD.**

Flying
Without wings
Arms outstretched
I hold my breath
Riding the currents of ecstasy
Waiting for that rip-cord moment
When rapid descent
Plunges me through the clouds
Of self-absorbed passion
Hallowing the hole in my soul
Satisfied in the soft landing of love

CHERRY PIE

Glistening lipstick
Tempts me
Brazen tart
I plunge my tines
Into crusty golden skin
Latticing
Your scarlet face
That fills me
With fruits of passion
Never enough

++++++++++++++++++++++++++++++++++++

When I first began writing I thought that all poetry had to rhyme. Learning the *freedom* of *free* verse (without meter) did *free* me for a whole new poetry experience. I still love rhyme, especially when it is humorous, but I find that I usually produce better poems when not having the restrictions of a rhyme scheme. The following poems with the one title came from trying both methods with the same silly subject. It is not a matter of which one is better but which do *you* like best?

STUFF (free verse)
Where did I get all this Stuff?
Did it drift with the sand through cracks in the door?
Stacks of inherited Stuff from parents and friends
who obviously couldn't take it with them
no matter how hard they tried.
I dust it, polish it, store it, cart it
across the country, then rearrange
my inventory in every new house.
Maybe I do need *some* Stuff after all.
Don't I sit on it, sleep in it,
wear *most* of it, constantly stare at it?
But, should I leave it to anyone I really *like*?

STUFF (rhyme)
Where did I get all this Stuff
that I now have to store?
Did it drift with the sand
through cracks in the door?
Stacks of inherited Stuff
from relatives who had to decide
they couldn't take it with them
no matter how hard they tried.
I cart it across the country
to each new depository,
dust and polish then
rearrange my inventory.
Maybe I do need
some Stuff after all.
I sit on it, wear it,
hang it from the wall.
Now, of course,
what I really want to know,
do I leave it to people I *like*
for *their* relatives to show?

125

FIGHTING BULL AT THE OPERA

Carmen toreadors in my ears
as I exit the Met,
opera breath
vibrating in video
steams the cold air.
Ignoring the rain,
I plunge into its icy knuckles
rush mob-like
past Manhattan's elegant
towards the conga line
of spitting yellow cabs.
Umbrella and high heels
swashbuckling any elbow
or shin that gets in my way,
I thrust and leap like Carmen's lover
fighting the bull.
If only I had a red cape
I would show these New Yorkers
how a California matador spears a cabbie.

FASHION POLICE

When I see beauty I want to cheer
When I see ugly I want to call 911

Since your ensemble affects me
More than it affects you
I say color coordinate your couture
For cultural coexistence

You say it is vanity to dress for success
I say it is a contribution to cohabitation
You say mirror mugging is unlawful
I say image improvement protects the public

Arrest those sweat panted
Tee-shirted tennie-footed
Senior teeny boppers in every mall
And support local fashion enforcement

Then just maybe I'll show you mine
If you'll show me yours

I happen to feel that if you are a poet, you can pretty much write anything—if you want to. Poetry got me started writing and continues to be my first love but I have also begun to try other creative genres as the following essay shows. Many famous authors began their careers with writing poetry. Even some journalists who are required to stick to facts in reporting often find an innovative outlet in writing poetry.

Maybe my emails and letters will be more interesting now that I debate with myself over every word I choose. I want to make sure that the same dull words I have used over and over, such as *cute, darling,* and *great* are replaced with more specific and varied language. I practically go to bed with my Synonym Finder.

Any story, whether truth or fiction, is more interesting when it includes imagery, metaphors, and novel language—all the things that are essential in good poetry. Do you suppose that is why a book of fiction is called a novel? How *novel*!

When I read prose and come upon a poetic phrase or an unusual figure of speech, I stop and wonder how in the world the author thought of such a jewel. I compare it to finding a sweet note from a friend tucked under the windshield wiper of my car— an unexpected personal gem. (Now, how is that for a comparison?) Many times I have set a book aside after only a few pages because unimaginative writing or clichés cluttered the message.

In whatever art form you choose to express yourself, it will be right for YOU. It doesn't have to be for anyone else in the world. That, to me, is the freedom of creativity.

CHANGING STRIPES

When my daughter announced that she was getting married, all I could think of was: *But he is a construction worker and in a union, for heavens sake!* My Republican, corporate wife status seemed threatened. *He is probably even a Democrat,* I thought—but didn't say—or maybe I did. *Aren't those the people who want the government to do everything for them?* I was horrified. So was her father.

Of course, I had seen my husband grow from a Mid-western farm boy, Roosevelt-Democrat, to vice-president of an oil company, Reagan-Republican, and we both had learned to rather like our new classy lifestyle. We weren't too concerned with blue-collar problems and I certainly loved my female role as wife and mother. The only titled position I might possibly be interested in adding would be grandmother. We supported all the "correct" political action committees—ones that had our best interest printed in their mission statement.

So, I choked back my snob bile, swallowed my own better lawyer choice and planned a wedding. My husband and I took our daughter and her boyfriend to an elegant restaurant for dinner to celebrate their engagement—me, hoping my son-in-law-to-be would know which fork to use. He did—my daughter did not. I couldn't believe I actually liked this guy. I saw how much he loved my child and how hard he worked so I decided maybe there was hope after all.

Surprisingly (at least to me), he had saved enough money since graduating from high school so they were able to move into their own home after the honeymoon. I even had to acknowledge (grudgingly) how much the union supported him, especially when the weather was bad and the jobs stopped or when a company didn't give proper compensation. I had not known that. He paid his dues and was loyal to the union although he never had to go out on strike, to my everlasting "what-will-my-friends-think" gratitude!

Then I became a widow and for the first time in my life I was on my own and had to learn to take care of myself, handle my own finances, buy and sell a car, buy and sell a house. I immediately realized that I was a single woman doing business in a white, male world. When I tried to get a credit card there was not even a credit record so I had to turn to (that's right) my son-in-law for advice. When I sat in my first ever, automobile dealership trembling from the intimidation of a macho car salesman—yep, there was you-know-who to do the negotiating. When I made my first major move alone, he was there. Whenever I needed anything—he was there.

I began to see how people who have no voice need the help of people who do. All the conservative ideals that I had always felt so righteous about seemed to be less practical when it came to my own situation. I saw others, especially women and minorities, having to deal with the power of the Establishment much of the time, and maybe needing an extra boost, just as I had. I joined an organization that required its members to study and debate every side of an issue before the group would declare a national position. I found that it was impossible to have tunnel vision about anything controversial with such many-sided, expanded views. My social conscience (or lack thereof) felt cramped and terribly uncomfortable, like too-tight pantyhose. I started shedding the weight of judgmental thinking and feasted instead on shifting attitudes. The old labels dropped away and my new stripes were actually painted LIBERAL.

Meanwhile back at the construction site, my son-in-law was also making the big leap—in the opposite direction. He was able to start his own business beginning with a tiny cement mixer that I gave them one Christmas. Borrowing a small amount of money and working from 5 a.m. to whenever the work was done, his company has grown into a major commercial enterprise with 78 employees. Although—get this—it is non-union! I guess, since he treats his people with such "I've-been-there" fairness and generosity, they feel no need. He now thinks and acts like a corporate magnate pulling in business with skill and style as if he has been an executive all his life. He has even initiated a program for local high schools to teach the masonry trade and also speaks to inmates in state prison about learning a vocation in order to help them find a job after release. I have watched this young man prove the adage that when you have something to conserve, that is when you color yourself CONSERVATIVE.

So here we are again—looking at each other from opposite sides of the political fence—but with amazing respect for the new and varied colors of our switched stripes.

END OF THE BRIDGE

Isn't it exhilarating to know that when there is another current to cross there will always be a bridge? I know there may be times when we look at a new challenge, whether it appears as a tiny trickling stream or a monstrous river, and think we just cannot cross one more bridge. But, of course we can and, we are *not* going to drown! We may not even get our feet wet, especially when we listen to that inner voice that tells us how to, what to, when to, where to, and maybe even who and why.

My bridges become steppingstones as I learn the wisdom of putting my insight, inspiration, hope, and fear—even my anger—into some kind of poetic form. To be healed and creative at the same time is a double blessing.

I encourage you to try it for your own well being and the well being of those around you. Don't you dare be embarrassed or apologetic for at least trying to write a poem! To lay our feelings out there for all to see and judge takes great courage. One of the biggest benefits of my new life is having reached the point where I am no longer so concerned with what others think. Learning to go from peace at any price to a sympathetic, yet assertive, woman is described by one friend as "unleashing a feminine monster." Oh, well, better a free-spirited individual than a veiled female waiting for approval.

I salute you for finishing this book. It shows impressive character when you invest time and effort into appreciating an unfamiliar art form. In the Bible when there is a major shift in character there is also a name change. Thus your new name is POET—or at least—POETRY ADVOCATE....

DESSA

STILL ON THE ROAD

ABOUT THE AUTHOR

Dessa Byrd Reed was born in Charleston, Illinois. She attended Eastern Illinois State College and the University of Illinois. Dessa and her late husband moved to California many years ago where she has had several careers including homemaker, advertising representative for an international newspaper, interior designer, practitioner for her church, as well as chaplain in two county jails.

After seeing the benefits of writing poetry in her own recovery, she now teaches poetry workshops and speaks to organizations encouraging others to find inspiration and direction in creating their own verse. Dessa Reed also sponsors poetry contests in several local schools helping young people discover their poetic voice and communicate their feelings.

DEER PUBLISHING
Post Office Box 3144
Palm Desert, California 92261

DessaReed@aol.com
www.dessabyrdreed.com

Dessa Byrd Reed
is also the author of

THE BUTTERFLY TOUCH
Recovery Through Poetry